STOP STRUGGLING
WITH YOUR TEEN

By

Evonne Weinhaus
and
Karen Friedman

Illustrations by Coral Goldenhersh

PUBLISHED BY J. B. SPECK PRESS

6345 Alexander

St. Louis, MO. 63105

ISBN 0-9613736-2-8

Cover design by Diane M. Beasley
Cover photo by Christopher Pruett

DEDICATION

This manual is based on the work of Drs. Bob and Jean Bayard, authors of How To Deal With Your Acting-Up Teenager. Working with Bob helped us find an approach to parenting that blends a calm, caring attitude with a determination to protect parental rights. Bob and Jean have touched the lives of many grateful parents and teens, and they have touched our lives as well. We want to thank them both for their inspiration.

ACKNOWLEDGMENTS

We would like to thank Judy and Perry Siegel for all their patience, Karen Kotner for her insight and direction, Sissy Hessler and Shel Weinhaus for their undaunting encouragement, Chuck Friedman for his lack of negativism, Judy Meyer for her editing suggestions, and of course our clients.

FOREWORD

Many books describe the plight of the parent-adolescent relationship, few however provide as clear a step-by-step means for effectively changing it as <u>Stop Struggling With Your Teen</u>. Evonne and Karen's manual outlines clear, concise, practical instructions on how to communicate with a teen without fighting.

I recommend this book to <u>all</u> parents. Those now struggling with teens can benefit immediately. Parents of younger children can get a head start on utilizing the techniques and concepts that promote a positive parent-child relationship. As a parent and therapist, I can assure you this book will help.

Laura Herring, M.A.Ed.
Marriage and Family Therapist

To order <u>Stop Struggling With Your Teen</u> send your check for $8.45 (includes postage and handling; Missouri residents please add $.42 sales tax) payable to:

J. B. SPECK PRESS
P. O. Box 9138
Richmond Heights, MO 63117

30 day money back guarantee

For special discount on bulk rate, or information regarding speaking engagements, please write to:

J. B. SPECK PRESS
6345 Alexander Drive
St. Louis, MO 63105

CONTENTS

CHANGING
YOUR ATTITUDE

In the Beginning

Binding Your Happiness To Your
Teen's Behavior

Translating Questions and
Accusations

CHAPTER I - CHANGING YOUR ATTITUDE

In The Beginning

The parent-teen relationship is unpredictable—so unpredictable it can turn your whole family upside down. You may find it comforting to know that most teenagers come out of the adolescent period right-side up. But in the meantime, many parents find themselves in a confusing and frustrating position. They have tried everything to create a healthy and harmonious atmosphere, but, for reasons they can't understand, they end up living in turmoil. Both adults and adolescents are left feeling discouraged and defeated.

As a parent, you may have tried some of the following methods of discipline:

GROUNDING: "You stayed out past curfew again. Now you're grounded for the week."

REWARDS: "I'll give you $15 for every 'A' you get."

GUIDANCE: "If you don't do your homework, you'll flunk out. Then you won't be able to get a good-paying job."

SUPERVISION: "I am going to take you to and from school every day and check with your teachers once a week."

UNDERSTANDING: "Why do you do these things? Let's talk about it so I can understand what's going on."

ORDERS: "Take the garbage out now."

PLEADING: "I don't ask that much from you. Please take your dirty dishes out of the den."

If you've found that some of these approaches work well with your teenager, stick with them! Don't tamper with success! However, if these methods aren't working and you are at your wits' end, it may be time to take a look at what's going on.

More than likely you have been doing one or both of the following:

1) Trying to run your teenager's life.

2) Failing to make your own life happy.

In this manual, we will give you a plan to turn this situation around. We would like for you to take each step seriously and spend some time on it. You might want to browse through the manual first to get an idea of the total picture, but then we recommend sitting down and working through each step in order. It seems reasonable that you should see some changes within six to eight weeks. As you continue to incorporate the ideas presented in this manual, you will not only see improvement, but in addition, both you and your teenager will gain a sense of self-satisfaction. You deserve the chance to be calm and happy, and your teenager deserves the chance to learn that he can be self-sufficient and run his own life.

Binding Your Happiness To Your Teen's Behavior

We will begin by taking a look at how you may have stopped taking care of yourself, because, before changing your relationship with your teen, you have to

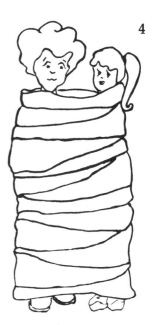

help yourself feel better. **All too often feelings of happiness are replaced with guilt, worry, and frustration that can accompany parenting. When this happens, parents develop an attitude that <u>binds</u> their happiness to the teenager's behavior.**

Some parental attitudes that can tie you to your teenager in this way are:

1) I'm always here to serve.
2) He's too young to use sound judgment.
3) What will other people think?
4) My kid is like a ball of clay that has to be molded.

These attitudes assume that you are entirely in charge of your child's actions, and that the teen is not capable of being responsible. When you see things this way, you put your own thoughts, feelings and wishes aside, and respond only to what your teen needs. Ultimately, you can end up sacrificing your own serenity and happiness.

Here's an example of what we are talking about:

Let's say your teenager makes a habit of arriving late for dinner because he has been out cruising with "undesirable" friends. You dutifully serve his dinner when he arrives home late as you complain about HIS tardiness and HIS choice of friends.

PARENT: "Where were you?"

TEEN: NO ANSWER.

PARENT: "Why didn't you call?"

TEEN: "I lost track of the time."

PARENT: "What do you mean you lost track of
               the time? You know you're supposed to
               be home at six.   You're getting as
               irresponsible as those so-called 'friends'
               of yours."

Notice where the focus is. It is on your teen! How do
you turn that situation around and focus on you?

You begin by realizing that although you may not be
able to control many aspects of your teenager's
behavior, you are in control of your own actions.
Therefore, instead of putting all your efforts into
"convincing" your child to change, you make an impact
by concentrating on what YOU can do.

Using the above situation as an example, you might substitute the dialogue with, "I am serving dinner at 6:30, and after that I am off duty." As you can see, this new statement changes the focus from "what the teen did" to "what I can do."

We have changed the focus by replacing questions and accusations that spotlight your teen's behavior with a simple direct statement that puts the spotlight on you and your action.

Translating Questions and Accusations

One way that you can begin to change the focus is by limiting your questions for one week. If you find this impossible, try one day at first. Don't give up—you can learn to replace many questions with statements about your own behavior—as we did in the example—and you may find that some questions aren't even necessary.

Let's look at the following for some additional examples.

Instead of asking questions:

"Why didn't you fill the car with gas before returning it?"

"Why do you always leave dirty dishes in the den?"

Try these statements:

"I want the gas tank to be filled when you use the car."

"I expect the dirty dishes to be put in the dishwasher."

Instead of making accusations:

"How dare you run up a huge telephone bill with all your long distance calls!"

"You should've told me earlier that you needed your baseball uniform washed by this afternoon."

Try these statements:

"I see your part of the telephone bill is $15.00, and I'd like it to be paid by the end of the week."

"I want 24-hour notice when you expect clothes cleaned by a certain time."

or

"I do not have time to take care of it."

Your decision to focus on your own behavior is a significant beginning in changing the parent-teen relationship. Your sense of powerlessness and helplessness will start to lift as you take control of your own behavior, and the hostile exchanges between you and your teen will diminish.

SUMMARY

Changing Your Attitude:

1)   Stick with the parenting approaches that have been working for you.

2)   Develop a new attitude that relieves you from feeling totally responsible for your teen's behavior.

3)   Realize that your happiness does not have to be bound to your teen's behavior.

4)   Change the emphasis from "what the teen did" to "what I can do."

LETTING GO

Kid Life Problems

Letting Go of Kid Life Problems

When Your Teenager Baits You

Asserting Yourself on Your
Part of the Problem

CHAPTER II – LETTING GO

Kid–Life Problems

We are now ready to begin. Write out a list of things that your teenager does that bother you. This list will be the basis of the work in this manual, and we hope to help you come up with a plan of action for each item on your list.

Let's say these are some of your problems:

- mistreats my personal belongings
- won't go to school
- doesn't do household chores
- lies to me
- wears ragged clothes
- uses drugs
- blasts stereo at all hours
- doesn't complete homework
- leaves messes everywhere
- is belligerent to me
- won't clean his room

Let's divide the problems into two lists. As you look it over, ask yourself what items <u>primarily</u> affect your kid's life and not yours. These kinds of problems

- doesn't complete homework
- wears ragged clothes
- won't go to school
- uses drugs
- won't clean his room

will be grouped together, and will be called Kid-Life problems.

You will notice that many of the items on the Kid-Life list do affect you in some way. Later on in the manual we will help you determine how to deal with the part of the problem that affects you directly, but for now, let's turn our attention to the teen's problems.

We suggest that you let go of trying to control your teen's behavior and turn the responsibility of these Kid-Life problems over to your child. Your immediate response to this idea may be, "There is no way I can

allow my child to decide by himself.   Those kind of
decisions could affect his entire future."

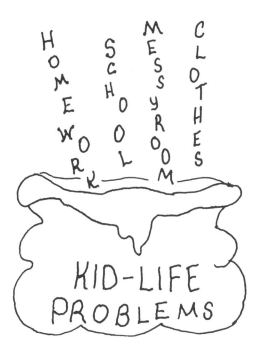

This is an understandable response, particularly because
parents believe it is their job to protect their child
from the hardships that the teen can bring on himself.
However, this kind of attitude can move parents to take

full responsibility for all of their kid's decisions. **Ultimately, they can make the mistake of confusing love for their child with how much they do for their child.** They make themselves available to help in any way possible, and soon both the parent and teen end up expecting the parent to be the problem-solver.

The teen leaves the worrying to the parent while he enjoys the light-hearted feeling of being irresponsible. It's easy to fall into this habit, but by doing this, you deprive the child of the security of knowing that he can find solutions to his own problems. You deprive him of:

> 1) the excitement and pride he can feel when complimented on his decisions
>
> 2) the lesson he can learn from his mistakes.

By helping less you allow your teen to test his own decision-making and to learn that he can count on himself and begin to take command of his own life.

When you turn responsibility over to your teen, you are showing faith in his ability. Your faith is the greatest form of encouragement for him to grow into a healthy, responsible adult.

Letting Go Of Kid-Life Problems

When you start to let go of Kid-Life problems, don't PANIC—you don't have to let go all at once. Think of it as an experiment.

First, choose a problem, one that is clearly a Kid-Life problem and would be easy for you to let your teenager handle without your involvement. When you let go of the problem, you will also let go of scolding, disapproving, advice-giving, and other attempts to control him. It is important to begin with "minor" issues so that you can live with your child's decision. If you initially choose a critical item, you may find it very difficult not to intervene in your child's decision-making.

Some examples of Kid-Life problems that parents might
turn over to their teen are the teen's choice of clothes
or the way he keeps his room.

Instead of using these situations to assert your control
over your teen, usually with little or no effect, you can
see them as an opportunity to recognize your child's
decision-making ability. For some parents, having a

neat room or being properly dressed are very important issues. If this is the case in your household, begin with a different Kid-Life problem. As we stated previously, it's essential that you choose something that is comfortable for you.

As parents let go of more significant Kid-Life problems, they may begin to feel worried or fearful of the choices their teens make. This is perfectly natural because parents want only what is best for their children. However, in wanting the best, parents sometimes forget that there are limits to what they can do. They frustrate themselves by believing that if they do the "right thing," the child will do what is "right." This can lead parents down a path of trying numerous approaches to reach the child. If each new attempt fails, parents may feel more frustrated and assert more control over the teen. What can eventually happen is that the parents find themselves in a paralyzing struggle with their teen, and little gets accomplished regarding the problem. By letting go of the Kid-Life problem, a parent can let go of the power struggle. **He can allow the teen to struggle constructively with the issue rather than struggle with the parent.**

A major Kid-Life problem that many parents find difficult to let go of is supervising their children's homework. This is due to the fact that achieving at school seems so bound up with a child's future. Parents put themselves in the uncomfortable position of policing this activity and scrutinizing the teen's every move. They don't allow the child to experience the consequences of receiving poor grades (e.g., summer school, ineligibility for extracurricular activities).

Here's an example of what happens in many households regarding this issue:

Mr. C. did everything possible to help his child develop good study habits. In an effort to make his reluctant daughter do her homework, he tried many tactics. He sat with her each evening to make sure the assignments were completed. He insisted that she have a two-hour study period in her room without interruptions from the telephone, stereo, or television, and finally he grounded her and withdrew her privileges. Mr. C's daughter thwarted him every step of the way. She "forgot" to bring home her assignments; she fell asleep on her bed during the study period, and she began lying and sneaking out of the house. Mr. C. knew he was beaten. He had started out as the taskmaster and ended up the slave to his child's decision about her homework.

He was ready to give up his job of policing and turn over the responsibility to his teen. He said:

> "I feel worn out trying to get you to do homework. I'm exasperated because nothing I've done has worked. From now on, I'm not going to interfere with your homework. I know you're capable, and I know you'll do what's right for you."

By making this statement, Mr. C removed himself from a power struggle that he felt he could never win. While he continued to want his daughter to do her homework, he realized that he could not force her. Therefore he changed his course of action and stopped struggling with his teen. What he did instead was state his position in a calm clear manner without making accusations or demands.

The communication skills used in this statement were organized by Robert and Jean Bayard, the authors of

How to Deal with Your Acting-Up Teenager, M. Evans and Company. Let's take a closer look at them.

Letting Go of the Responsibility

Communication skills:	Examples:
STATE your feelings and thoughts.	I feel worn out trying to get you to do homework. I'm exasperated because nothing I've done has worked.
TURN OVER the responsibility.	From now on, I'm not going to interfere with your homework.
SHOW trust.	I know you're capable, and I know you'll do what's right for you.

Notice that the statement is brief and clear, so that the teen will listen and understand. **It is important to let go of the problem in a way that reflects a loving, respectful attitude so that the teen realizes that you are giving him responsibility rather than just giving up.** In this way, letting go becomes another way that you can demonstrate your love for your child.

As we continue with the manual, we will be presenting additional skills that you may choose to incorporate when you turn over the responsibility. In addition, we will discuss in more detail how you can take action on issues that affect you, but for now, let's focus on what may happen after you turn over the responsibility.

When Your Teenager Baits You

Let's assume you have taken this first step of turning responsibility over to your teen. Then, guess what happens? Many kids act even worse than before. Look at it this way: If you had someone take responsibility for your life, would you suddenly be willing to give that up? Of course not -- at least not without a struggle.

So, your teenager may try to hook you into taking back
the responsibility.   Remember, teenagers can be
experts at dangling the bait.

Before you know it, you may find yourself responding to
questions such as:

"Did anything from school come in the mail?"

"Did my teacher call you?"

Step back for a moment so you can begin to realize what is going on. Now it is your teenager who is asking the questions. He is even broaching a subject that may spell trouble for him. This is your cue that you have succeeded. He is experiencing the discomfort that can come with taking on responsibility, and he wants to dump it back into your lap.

His questions and comments are inviting you to take back his responsibilities and play the role of the bad guy. He is testing you, and this time you're ready for him. You will no longer allow your teen to cast you in the role of villain—no matter how hard he tries.

PARENT: "Yes, the mail came, and you received a notice from school."

TEEN: "Didn't you open it?"

PARENT: "No, here it is. Also, the teacher called to tell me you missed three assignments last week."

TEEN: "I really meant to get them in on time, but I just didn't have time."

PARENT: "When I first found out, I was upset because I had hoped you'd buckle down at school. At this rate, you may end up in summer school or be left back and not have any education or skills to find a job."

TEEN: "What are you going to do about it?"

PARENT: "I don't know. I understand that you feel pressured. I would like you to do well in school, but I realize I can't make you study. However, I'd be willing to help you in some reasonable way."

TEEN: "Well, I will have all of my homework done by tomorrow."

PARENT: "That is up to you. I know you will do what's good for you. I do want you to know that I told your teacher today that I'm not going to sign your assignment sheets."

TEEN: "You told Mr. Jones that! You can't do that—the school said that you have to check and sign my assignment sheets."

PARENT: "After we talked, we agreed that my signing your assignment sheets has not been helpful. So I'm not going to sign your work anymore, and the school understands what I'm doing."

Let's review the skills used in this dialogue.

Helpful Communication Skills

Communication skills:	Examples:
DESCRIBE only what you see without judging.	The mail came, and you received a notice from school. Also, the teacher called to tell me you missed three assignments last week.

STATE your feelings and thoughts.	When I first found out, I was upset because I had hoped you would buckle down at school.
POINT out possible consequences.	At this rate, you may end up in summer school, or be left back and have no education or skills to find a job.
RECOGNIZE teen's feelings.	I understand that you feel pressured.
EXPRESS what you want while acknowledging your lack of control.	I would like you to do well in school, but I realize I can't make you study.
OFFER some help.	I'd be willing to help you in some reasonable way.
SHOW trust.	I know you will do what's good for you.

ADDRESS the part of the problem that affects you directly.

"After we talked, we agreed that my signing your assignment sheets has not been helpful. So I'm not going to sign your work anymore, and the school understands what I'm doing."

This last statement deals with the part of the problem that affects you. While it is important to encourage your child to take responsibility for his behavior, it is just as important to recognize and attend to your part of the problem. Here you can begin to exert your energy and your rights in a respectful, fruitful way. Let's take a closer look at your part of the problem.

Asserting Yourself on Your Part of the Problem

Often parents work so hard at trying to control the entire Kid-Life problem that they are not able to

separate out the part of the problem that directly
affects them. They spend all their energy trying to tell
their teen what to do and are left feeling too drained to
assert their own rights. By addressing the part of the
problem that does affect them, parents not only take
control of themselves, but also integrate respect for
the child's decision with respect for their own values.
To show how you can attend to your part of the
problem, we will turn our attention to truancy--an issue
that clearly affects both teen and parent.

Let's take the case of Mrs. J. The more her son missed
school, the more angry and frustrated Mrs. J. became.
She made numerous attempts to get her son to go to
school, but none of her efforts seemed to make an
impact.

Mrs. J. knew she had to do something different. Her
last-ditch effort was to escort her son to and from
school daily. She reorganized her days around her

son's school schedule. It did not work. Her son just left
school as soon as he saw the car pull away. Mrs. J. felt
that she had exhausted every possible option; she was
emotionally and physically drained. She was ready for a
change; Mrs. J. was ready to take the burden off of her
own shoulders and place it where it rightfully belonged
— on her son.

Using the communication skills already mentioned, she
turned over the responsibility to her child and asserted
herself on the parent's part of the problem.

> "I have been worried about you not going
> to school, and I feel frustrated about
> what to do. I know you've been feeling
> hassled by me. From now on, it's up to
> you to work out your attendance record
> with the school.   I want you to know
> that I will not talk to school officials
> without your participation.

Let's review some of the communication skills we have
previously discussed:

Communication skills:	Examples:
STATE your thoughts and feelings.	I have been worried about you not going to school, and I feel frustrated about what to do.

RECOGNIZE   teen's   I know you've been feeling
feelings.   hassled by me.

TURN   OVER   the   From now on, it's up to you
responsibility.   to work out your attendance
                         record with the school.

ADDRESS your part   I want you to know that I will
of the problem.   not talk to school officials
                         without your participation.

Again, the questions and accusations that are typically
spoken by parents, "Why didn't you go to school?...You'll
never amount to anything" are replaced with specific
observable, nonjudgmental statements. The unheeded
advice, "You should go to school" is replaced with a
clear, concise statement about your own action.

Another example of a problem that affects both teens
and parents is <u>sexual activity.</u> Like truancy, it is of
great concern to parents, and it is impossible to
monitor or control. Typically, parents deal with this by
using everything from reasoning to locking the teen in
the bedroom, only to find that when the teen has the
will, there's a way. It's understandable that most
parents with only the best of intentions try everything
they can think of to change the teen's attitude and
behavior, especially on critical issues such as this one.
However, if the teen is determined, the parent is left
with little recourse—and usually ends up feeling
thoroughly hopeless and angry.

Rather than try to enforce the impossible, parents can:

1) Turn over the responsibility to their teen.

> "I don't agree with your level of sexual
> activity, and I'm afraid of what might
> happen. I imagine that you could end up
> pregnant. I hope you decide not to have
> sex, but there's nothing I can do about it.

From now on, I'm not going to monitor
your sexual activity."

2) Take a stand on the Parent-Life issue.
"I do not want you sleeping with your
boyfriend in my house, or entertaining
him   in your bedroom with the door
closed. Also, I want you to know, if you
should become pregnant, I will not raise
a grandchild."

The parent sticks to the aspect of the problem that
affects his life directly.   There are no lectures, no
sermons, and no reprimands.

One final example of a problem that affects both teens
and their parents is chemical dependency.   Due to the
special nature of this problem, we would recommend
getting professional help if you suspect that you teen is
abusing drugs. For those who have teens who seem to
defy all attempts to help them, we suggest that you
begin to make some changes by using the ideas that we
have set forth in this manual:

1) Turning over the responsibility to your teen

2) Taking a stand on your part of the problem

You can begin to turn over the responsibility to your teen by allowing him to experience the consequences of his drug-related behavior. For example, if your teen drives his car into a ditch, leave it there; if your teen becomes sick, let him clean up his mess. By leaving the evidence of his chemical dependency, you make it more difficult for him to deny the problem. Breaking down the denial system that surrounds this illness is often the first step towards getting help.

Another way to refuse to cooperate with your teen's drug use is to take a stand where you do have control. Even though you can't stop your teen from taking drugs when he is away from home, you can take action where you are directly involved. You can insist that your home is free from drugs and paraphernalia, or you can refuse to bail your child out of the trouble his drug-use creates. In this way you make a firm commitment to assert your rights and expectations where your life is affected without trying to control the entire problem.

This approach may not change the teen's drug use. However, if you are going to live under the same roof with your teen in spite of his refusal to stop using drugs, you need to know that you are doing all you can.

SUMMARY

Letting Go of Kid-Life Problems:

1)   Turn over the responsibility.

2)   Avoid your teen's baiting you into taking back the responsibility.

3)   Express your views and feelings and offer encouragement.

4)   Address your part of the problem.

TAKING
A STAND

Asserting Parental Rights
The Four Steps

CHAPTER III - TAKING A STAND

Asserting Parental Rights

Thus far we have discussed how you can let go of Kid-Life problems and allow consequences to teach your child the importance of responsible decision-making.

We will spend the remainder of the manual on presenting ways for parents to take a stand on Parent-Life problems. This process can bring about a much improved relationship with your teen and a better feeling about yourself. We would like to suggest that you spend several weeks, making the shift into standing up for yourself on Parent-Life problems because you are working toward a very basic change in the parent-teen relationship. Remember—it took your child many years of practice to become such an expert at giving excuses when you ask him to do something. Give yourself a break, and realize it will take some time to change things. Keep the faith—it will work!

Let's go back to the original list and separate out the Parent-Life problems:

- blasts stereo at all hours
- mistreats my personal belongings
- doesn't do household chores
- leaves messses everywhere
- lies to me
- is belligerent to me

You may find that some of the Parent-Life problems, particularly those that center around your teen's attitude:

- lies to me
- is belligerent to me

have already diminished since you let go of Kid-Life problems. Quite simply, when parents stop playing detective by asking too many questions and stop making derogatory comments about their kids' behavior, teenagers do not have as much occasion to substantiate their case with lies and defensive maneuvers.   In addition, when parents demonstrate faith in their children's decision-making abilities, teenagers often respond to this as a form of encouragement and act accordingly.

However, it is almost a sure bet when it comes to a major change of the teen's behavior, you probably will have an opportunity to practice the following four steps organized by Robert and Jean Bayard in <u>How to Deal with Your Acting-Up Teenager:</u> negotiate an agreement, insist with persistence, take action, and arrange a limited strike.

The Four Steps

STEP ONE—Negotiate an Agreement

You are going to begin to negotiate an agreement with your teen around a Parent-Life issue. It is essential that you begin your work by taking one specific example of a Parent-Life problem. First, decide which one you want to tackle.

Here are some examples of clear-cut Parent-Life issues:

Your teenager blasts his stereo from the moment he gets home until he goes to bed, your head is in pain, and there is no relief from the noise.

Your child has to have a pair of jeans washed and dried immediately and takes your clothes out of the dryer so he can dry his. Yours are left dripping wet.

Your teenager decides he must have a snack, and then leaves every bit of evidence present to greet you when you walk into the kitchen.

You want help bringing in the groceries, and everyone seems to disappear from sight.

It is quite possible that on some issues you will be able to take care of your needs by making a clear statement of your expectations:

> "When you listen to your stereo in your room, I want your door closed so I don't hear the music."

> "When you take my clothes out of the dryer, put them back and make sure the dryer is turned on."

> "When you fix yourself a nightime snack, please clean up the kitchen."

Your teen may go along with you because you're taking care of yourself without limiting his needs. Your rights can coexist with those of your teen.

However, if you're still having difficulty, try the following communication skills. We will use the example of bringing in the groceries, but these skills can be used with other Parent-Life issues as well.

Negotiate an Agreement

<u>Communication skills:</u>   <u>Examples:</u>

MAKE a clear state-   I want a different way of
ment about what you   handling chores because I end
want and your will-   up doing all the work now. I
ingness to negotiate.   want to try to work out
                           something together.

STATE what you   I think it would be fair if I
think would be a fair   shopped for the groceries and
agreement.   you put them away.

WORK out a negotia-   When I shop I'll have them
tion with your teen,   bag the perishables and non-
using input from <u>both</u>   perishables separately.   I'll
of you.   After you   put away the perishables, and
reach an agreement,   you'll put away the non-
summarize.   perishables.

STEP TWO—Insist With Persistence

It is time now to test out your negotiated agreement. You may be one of the fortunate parents whose teenagers say, "Sure, no problem," and then completes his chore—but don't bank on it.   More than likely, your teenager will not change just because you successfully completed step one.   Your teenager will probably want to flex his muscles and test your firmness.

In the following conversation, the teenager refuses to bring in the groceries and also successfully maneuvers you into giving her attention for negative behavior.

You have gone shopping and you say, "The groceries need to be brought inside and put away."

TEEN: "Can't it wait until I'm off the phone?"

PARENT: "We made a deal.   It is obvious you don't remember."

TEEN: "Why don't you ask sis? She never does anything."

PARENT: "She just cleaned the dog messes YOU were supposed to do, but never got around to. Now get off the phone!"

TEEN: "All right, all right, just give me another minute. Isn't it important I get my homework assignment? You know you always say homework comes first."

PARENT: "Oh, all of a sudden you care about homework. That's a switch. You didn't seem to care last week when you didn't study for the exam you flunked."

TEEN: "You just don't understand. It wasn't my fault. Most of the other kids flunked too. It was an unfair test!"

PARENT: (Ten minutes later) "Get off that phone NOW!"

TEEN: "I said I will in a minute!"

PARENT: (Yelling) "So help me, I will disconnect
                   the phone!"

Five minutes later the parent disconnects the phone,
the teenager runs out of the house screaming that no
one cares what happens to her, and the groceries are
still in the car.

The child has successfully made herself look like the
victim and avoided doing the chore. You feel angry,
frustrated and defeated, and to make matters worse,
you end up putting the groceries away. Is there no
justice in the world?

In the next example, the teenager still doesn't put away
the groceries, but she does not successfully bait you
into giving her attention or getting you off the track.

TEEN: "Can't it wait until I'm off the phone?"

PARENT: "I see you're on the phone—and—I want
                 the groceries put away."

TEEN: "Why don't you ask sis? She never does
                 anything."

PARENT: "I know you think I should ask your
                 sister—and—I want the groceries put
                 away."

TEEN: "All right, all right, just give me
                 another minute. Isn't it important I get
                 my homework assignment? You know
                 you always say homework comes first."

PARENT: "I know you are getting your homework
                 assignment—and—I want the groceries
                 put away."

You're not justifying, you're not defending your position, and you're not emphatically claiming you have a fair and caring attitude. Your statements demonstrate that you heard what she said, and at the same time you are sticking to accomplishing what you want. You stay on the task despite your teen's valiant effort to get you off track.

The skill that is used in this instance is a three-part assertive statement: "I know you would like to finish your phone conversation, <u>and</u> I want the groceries put away."

Three-Part Assertive Statement

Communication skills:	Examples:
SUMMARIZE calmly what your teen said.	I know you would like to finish your telephone conversation
USE the word "and"	AND

instead of the word
"but" to demonstrate
that   your   teen's
needs and your needs
can coexist.

MAKE a short state-   I want the groceries put
ment expressing what   away.
you want.

Don't become discouraged. Even if the short-range goal
of putting away the groceries was not achieved, you
have accomplished the goal of taking care of yourself in
a respectful manner. You have made this step a
success if you have been persistent in a polite and
relaxed manner, and if you have not become
sidetracked by answering questions or scolding.
Remember, you may need to try this step two or three
times before you see any results.

STEP THREE—Take Action

If you continue to let go of Kid-Life problems while you
begin to take care of your needs, you should see some

improvement in your teen's willingness to cooperate with you. If not, it's possible that your teenager still may not believe that you really will stand up for yourself. Is he going to be in for some surprises when you start step three.

Step three is a move designed to establish in your teenager's mind that you can be counted on to do what you say. This step is different from the first two because it moves you from talking into taking action. So, take a deep breath, and get ready for a shift to a new direction. You want to establish an entirely new notion—that you do what you say. This is called changing the balance of power, and this can be fun.

Here is how to go about it.

A.   State what you want using a calm, relaxed statement that keeps the focus on the issue.

> "I want the nonperishables put away within the next hour."

"I will pay you for mowing the lawn, and
I want it done by Friday."

"I don't want your coat hung up on the
floor."

"I want your clean socks put away after I
do the laundry."

B. When the situation arises again, say what you are
going to if the task is not completed. **Choose an
action that is clearly related to the problem so that
your focus is on completing the task rather than
punishing your child:**

"If the nonperishables aren't put away,
I'm going to leave them in the car."

"If the lawn is not mowed by Friday, I
will pay the neighborhood boy to do it."

"If your coat is not hung up in the
closet, I will put a cardboard box
outside and toss your coat into it."

This step can be especially effective when you incorporate humorous, zany ideas into your action.

"If the socks are not put away by this evening, I will hang them on the chandelier."

C. Move into action.

> Now it's time to show that you can be counted on to do what you say by moving into action. Your intent is to establish your credibility, as well as to teach your teen to help with the chores. Keep in mind, you are working toward the long-range goal of being taken at

your word rather than teaching your
child a lesson or taking revenge.

STEP FOUR—Arrange a Limited Strike

By now, we think you will have found improvements in
your relationship with your teen. If, however, you have
systematically followed the steps in this manual and
still feel exasperated and defeated, it's time to take
away what kids can take for granted and move to step
four—limited strike. Sometimes it is very tempting to
move to this action without going through the first
three steps. DON'T! It assumes that negotiation will
not work between you and your teen.

What we are suggesting in step four is that you look
over the things you do for your child, things that may
be expected rather than appreciated. Find something
that you can stop doing for your teen. For example,
you can stop doing his laundry, cooking for one week,
chauffeuring, etc.

Don't be afraid to do something that will affect other family members. Be specific and set a clear time limit so everyone will know what to expect.

Once you have decided what action you will take, tell your teen in a short statement that keeps the focus on you.

> "I'm tired of doing all the work without help from others. I have decided not to cook dinner for the rest of the week. If I don't cook, then I don't have to worry about getting help bringing in the groceries."

> "I'm not doing your laundry for the rest of the month. I am going to use the time that I usually spend washing and ironing to do the yardwork because that has been neglected by you. I feel like I've been making all the compromises. Now I'm going to take care of things around the house that matter to me."

What you hope to accomplish with a limited strike is to demonstrate that you won't be taken for granted, and you will take care of yourself. More importantly, your teen can begin to experience the consequences when there is a lack of mutual cooperation in any relationship, and this is a great lesson.

SUMMARY

Taking a Stand on Parent-Life Problems:

1) Step one: Negotiate a fair deal with your teen that is agreeable to both of you.

2) Step two: If your teen doesn't honor the negotiation, be persistent using the three-part assertive statement.

3) Step three: Establish the credibility of your word by taking action.

4) Step four: Arrange a limited strike.

REVIEW

This section will give you an opportunity to review and practice some of the skills presented in this manual.

Here is a typical list of problems for you to work through.

Your teen:

- . monopolizes the telephone
- . stays up late
- . fights with siblings
- . takes your car without permission

Separate the Kid-Life and Parent-Life problems by asking yourself the following question:

Whose life is primarily affected—mine or my teenager's?

Now that you have divided the list, devise a method for dealing with each problem. We have come up with some suggested ideas, but remember there is no one right answer. Read through our first example and then try working on the others by yourself.

KID-LIFE PROBLEMS

Stays Up Late

Communication skills:	Examples:
STATE your feelings and thoughts.	I have been trying to get you to go to bed early, and I have ended up feeling frustrated.
SHOW trust.	I realize that you are capable of deciding how much sleep you need.
TURN OVER the responsibility.	From now on I will not interfere when you go to sleep or wake up.

REVIEW

Fighting Among Siblings

Communication skills:	Examples:
EXPRESS what you want while acknowledging your lack of control.	I wish the two of you would stop fighting with one another, but I realize I can't stop you.
POINT out possible consequences.	Sometimes I'm afraid that one of you will end up in the hospital with a broken arm.
TURN OVER the responsibility.	From now on I am going to stay out of your fights. It is up to you to work them out.
ADDRESS your part of the problem.	I want you to know that I will not pay for items broken due to your fighting. I expect all

loud fighting to be done
outside or in the basement so
I don't hear the noise.

PARENT-LIFE PROBLEMS

Takes the Car Without Permission

Communication skills:

Examples:

MAKE a clear state-
ment of what you
expect.

I expect you to ask permission when you want to use
the car. If I'm not asked, I
will not lend my car.

Monopolizes the telephone

Communication skills:

Examples:

STATE agreement.

If a family member is on the
telephone and someone else
wants to use it, the person on

the phone has ten minutes to end the conversation. Also, after 9:00 on school nights, the phone is reserved for adult use.

USE the three-part assertive statement

I understand this is an important call, and it is after 9:00 so it is my time.

OR

I know you have not finished your conversation yet, and your ten minutes are up.

TAKE action.

I expect the phone to be free at 9:00. If not, over the weekend I am going to disconnect all the phones except the one in my bedroom.

CONCLUSION

Now that you have read the manual, you may find yourself beginning to make some changes in your life.

We believe that when you:

- . show a caring attitude to your teen and yourself,

- . let your teen take responsibility for Kid-Life problems,

- . assert yourself on issues that directly affect you,

you and your teen have a much better chance of developing a cooperative relationship based on self-respect and respect for one another.

We hope you have learned that:

. turning over responsibility can be a great source of encouragement and demonstration of faith in your teenager's ability.

. allowing your teen to experience the consequences of his behavior can be a powerful teacher.

. taking a stand on Parent-Life issues minimizes your sense of helplessness.

With your new attitude you may begin to view your child as someone you can care about without being someone you have to mold. You will watch what he does with interest and begin to delight in watching him struggle with his decisions. Your new approach to problem-solving will broaden your options, recognize your needs, and above all, give your teen an opportunity to grow.

ABOUT THE AUTHORS

Evonne Weinhaus earned her B.A. from Washington University in St. Louis. After several years of teaching, she completed a Masters Degree in Education at Webster College and a Masters Degree in Counseling Psychology at the Alfred Adler Institute of Chicago. In addition to counseling families, she provides consultation and training to area schools, hospitals and professional organizations. Her commitment to parent education is reflected in her development and implementation of numerous parent study programs throughout the St. Louis community. She lives with her husband, Sheldon, and their three teenagers.

Karen Friedman received her B.A. from Hunter College in New York, an M.S.W. from the University of Missouri and has four years of post graduate work at the Alfred Adler Institute of Chicago. Her work with families began in 1974 as a clinician at St. Joseph's Hospital in Chicago. There she contributed to the development of a Family Education Program. Since her move to St. Louis, she has acted as consultant to community agencies, maintained a private practice and trained graduate students and professionals through local universities. She resides with her husband, Chuck, and their three children.